Plainsongs

Editor

Eric R. Tucker

Associate Editors

Becky Faber, Michael Catherwood,
Eleanor Reeds, Ali Beheler

Publisher

Patricia Oman, HC Press

Production Assistants

Hannah Gehle
Gideon Monette

Cover photo by Amy Sandeen

Hastings College Press | Hastings, Nebraska
https://www.hastings.edu/hastings-college-press/

Subscriptions to *Plainsongs* are $20.00 annually for two issues, published in January and July.

Plainsongs welcomes submissions. The manuscript deadline for the Spring/Summer 2021 issue is December 15, 2020. Contributors will receive one free copy of the issue in which their poem appears.

Please use our online submission manager, available on our website, to submit work. We cannot guarantee responses for work submitted through any other method. For more information about submitting poetry or subscribing to *Plainsongs*, please see our new website: https://www.corpuscallosumpress.com/plainsongs.

Plainsongs is indexed by Humanities International Complete, EBSCO Information Services, 10 Estes Street, Ipswich, MA 01938.

ISBN-13   978-1-942885-80-1

ISSN   1534-3820

Plainsongs

Winner of the Jane Geske Award,
presented by the Nebraska Center for the Book

Notes from the Editor

So much has happened since our last issue. The emergence (and potential reemergence) of a deadly pandemic. Widespread job loss and economic hardship. Hundreds of thousands of people in the streets, protesting racial injustice. We are living in tumultuous, dizzying, despairing times. We mourn the Black lives that have been senselessly snuffed out: those of George Floyd, Ahmaud Arbery, Breonna Taylor, James Scurlock, Rayshard Brooks, and so many others. We watch helplessly as severe coronavirus infections disproportionately befall the nonwhite, the elderly, and the disadvantaged. In the face of governmental inaction, we worry about our collective future on a perpetually warming planet. We are angry. We feel hollowed out. We long for change. Perhaps we are on the cusp of it. As we Zoom with loved ones and keep a safe distance from one another in grocery stores, peering suspiciously over the avocados at the unmasked among us, we search for signs—*any* signs—of hope. There have been glimmers. A historic Supreme Court decision confirming workplace protections for LGBTQ+ individuals. Another blocking the administration's attempt to end support for DACA recipients. An announcement by the NFL reversing its opposition to players' kneeling in protest of tragic police killings of Black people. We cling to hope wherever we can find it: in sports, in avocados, in poetry.

If not sports or avocados, we can at least provide the poetry. In this second issue of volume 40, you will find award-winning poems by Joshua Michael Stewart, Mike Frenkel, and Elizabeth Stoessl, along with insightful essays by associate editors Eleanor Reeds, Michael Catherwood, and Becky Faber. You will find a stunning cover image by Amy Sandeen. You will find poems of protest; you will find humor; you will find moments of reflection; you will find images of sublime beauty. Perhaps in these pages you will find a turn of phrase or an arresting poetic image that gives you something akin to hope.

Of course, between the writing of these notes and the publication of *Plainsongs*, countless other momentous events—some hopeful, some tragic—may have transpired. With any luck, the scales will tip in favor of the hopeful. For our part, we hope this issue finds you and your loved ones safe and well, and we thank you for your continued support of *Plainsongs* and of the arts.

Eric R. Tucker
Hastings, Nebraska

Contents

Elegy for Who I Once Was 10
    Joshua Michael Stewart
About "Elegy for Who I Once Was":
A *Plainsongs* Award Poem 11
    Eleanor Reeds
The Widening Gyre 12
    Mike Frenkel
About "The Widening Gyre":
A *Plainsongs* Award Poem 13
    Michael Catherwood
Coal Delivery Day, 1950 14
    Elizabeth Stoessl
About "Coal Delivery Day, 1950":
A *Plainsongs* Award Poem 16
    Becky Faber
The Forgotten War 17
    John Struloeff
Golem 18
    Mary Ann Dimand
Cultural Confusions 19
    Kieran Egan
Stowaway 20
    Devon Balwit
Grasslands 21
    Bonnie Larson Staiger
Keys 22
    Shannon K. Winston
Eve Reflects 24
    Cecilia Gigliotti
Storm Flow 25
    Robert Lee Kendrick
Dirty Laundry 26
    Megan Savage
The Lament of the First Chinese Brother 28
    Lisa Shirley
A Martini Over a Stone Floor 29
    Adela Najarro
The Map of the States 30
    Barbara Daniels
Leaving the Concert Hall 31
    Sean Lause
Andromeda 32
    Holly Day
Requiem, Father 33
    C. E. Greer
100 Blessings 34
    Alan Toltzis
Unknown Elegy 35
    Will Simescu

Moths 36
    C.M. Barnes
Taking Down the Clothes 37
    Anne Knowles
Our Daughter in Darkness 38
    Cecil Morris
Circle Dance 39
    Lin Marshall Brummels
The Fundamentals 40
    John Zedolik
Dirt Time 41
    Robert Rothman
How Much Does the Anne Frank House Cost? 42
    Sharon Kennedy-Nolle
Hoax 44
    Donna Pucciani
Palmyra, Illinois 46
    Jared M. Campbell
tortoise 47
    Genevieve Hartman
The White Season 48
    Miguel Eichelberger
For Samuel Morse 49
    Mark Christhilf
Self-portrait with Memory 50
    Marjorie Maddox
Hailstorm Disquiet 51
    Marilyn Dorf
White Buffalo Woman 52
    Wyle McClain
They Say of Rain 53
    Chet Corey
Forecast 54
    Francine Rubin
Ghost Leg 55
    Joseph Hardy
History Lessons 56
    Christopher Snook
Friends 57
    Mark Metcalf
LIFE and Ruby Bridges 58
    Calida Osti
Acroyoga 60
    Janis Harrington
Open 61
    Rachel Tramonte
Sun Salutation 62
    Kara Mae Brown
Poem for the Dog Jaya 63
    John Krumberger
The New Particle 64
    Todd Johnson

Water Ceremony 66
   Michael Phillips
Staggering Bees... 67
   Yvonne Higgins Leach
Is Pluto Still a Planet? 68
   Joan Colby
Abattoir... 69
   Marc Meierkort
Battle of Los Angeles, 2006 70
   Eric Kennedy
The Definition... 72
   Jayne Warren
Sediment Remains.. 73
   Samn Stockwell
Footfall.. 74
   Christopher Goedert
Lesson Learned... 76
   Patricia L. Hamilton
Hope.. 78
   Margo L. Foreman
Opportunity 79
   Maria Anderson Knudtson
Sourgrass and Tadpoles.. 80
   Robert Parham
My maiden aunts 81
   Ed Block
Stocking Shelves at Hills Supermarket—1974 82
   Geo. Staley
Cashier Strays from Register 84
   Dave Malone
Sometime After My Father Died 85
   Tate Lewis
In the Air 86
   Naomi Ruth Lowinsky
Secrets 88
   Carol Bason
Nothing 89
   Robert Cooperman
Just a Bite 90
   Lilian Bodley
Our City 92
   Steven Ray Smith
Northern Ringneck 93
   Ace Boggess
Childhood Enrichment 94
   Charlene Neely
Holly, Who Works Overnights at the Kwik Shop 95
   Cathy Porter
The Attic 96
   Krikor N. Der Hohannesian
Beginning.. 97
   Katherine Fallon

Blue Dress Wearing a Small Girl 98
    Karisma J. Tobin
No True Dark 99
    Caitlin Thomson
Summer Haibun 100
    Andrena Zawinski
Early Friday I Wondered, Suddenly, Was Cab Calloway Living, Was He Dead 101
    Lyn Lifshin
Who's Who 102
    John Grey
Even Out Back, I'd Travel with a Trowel 104
    Christine Butterworth-McDermott
For Mary Oliver 105
    Sasha Blakeley
New Roots 106
    Karen Poppy
What She Knows 107
    Princess Zuri' McCann
Lingering 108
    Julia Horensten
Unwritten 109
    Danielle Valverde
A Monologue of a Theater Teacher 110
    Sujash Purna
The Problem with Water 111
    B. Neal Kirchner
Some Things I've Not Done 112
    Florence Weinberger
Almost August 113
    Michael Lyle
Comfort at the Muzzleloader Café, Billings, Montana 114
    Linda Conroy
I Ask My Realtor How to Keep the Ghosts the Same 115
    Megan Mary Moore
Cradle of Moss 116
    Kathrine M. Cays
My Foolish Heart 117
    Abigail Warren
Survey 118
    Jonce Marshall Palmer
Pink Wheat 119
    Anna Ciummo
I Wish I Had Batman's Origin Story 120
    Keli Lindsey
Richard's Story 121
    Matthew J. Spireng
Buzz 122
    Mary Ann Meade

Elegy for Who I Once Was

Summer. We were walking
a country road before dawn
and you were dead.
I don't remember your dying
but there you were, dragging your feet,
your eyes like the bottoms of glass ashtrays.
Your breath.
I said it smelled of death
and you just groaned.
I felt like an idiot.
I never wanted this.
I never wanted it to rain.
Do you have any idea
what a soggy corpse is like
so early in the morning?
I tried to pick up the pace,
but all you could do was slosh down the road.
Eventually, we came to a barn
and hobbled inside to get dry.
Soon the sun was up. The rain had stopped
and the insects were getting jiggy in the fields.
You slumped into an empty stall.
Sunlight beamed through slits in the boards
and the dust of your body mingled
with the dust of the barn, the outside world
and possibly me. Despite the decay
you looked lovely disappearing like that.
And I confessed if I wasn't such a fool
I'd love you right down to the bone.
Vultures usually do.
It was the first thing you'd said all morning.

Joshua Michael Stewart
Ware, Massachusetts

About "Elegy for Who I Once Was": A *Plainsongs* Award Poem

The simplicity of this poem's opening sets the scene for a starkly physical encounter with the "soggy corpse" of the speaker's former self. The rhythm of the longer and shorter lines mimics his journey with such a burden as well as enabling the punch lines to land effectively. Joshua Stewart's use of sound also contributes to the dynamics of the poem: for example, the speaker "tried to pick up the pace" but this plosive energy was stalled by the onomatopoeic "slosh" of his companion.

The rhetorical question partway through the poem reminds us that its scene of address is necessarily triangulated: the poem is not consistently or solely addressed to the dead because it also appeals to the reader, who is asked to acknowledge the living man's difficult task and bear silent witness to his confession. However, the dead man speaks, without warning or introduction, in the penultimate line's bitter and humorous retort. The more meditative mood of the barn had transformed the "slump" of a rotting zombie into an angelic dissolve, but the pathos of the speaker's declaration of love "right down to the bone" is made brutally literal by the judgment of his former self.

Figurative images are scarce in "Elegy for Who I Once Was." The isolated simile, "your eyes like the bottoms of glass ashtrays," vividly adds to the literal weight of the confrontation between the "I" and the "you" of the poem, deepening the reader's attention to the material contrasts of air, water, and earth invoked by Stewart's references to breath, rain, dust, and bone. This is a poem that refuses all abstractions, providing a visceral reminder that who we once were leaves marks on both earth and flesh.

Eleanor Reeds
Hastings, Nebraska

The Widening Gyre

We are walking in the park,
me along the outer track,
six times around.
She takes the inner path
once around the lake.
She is hunched over,
leans heavily on her walker,
stops from time to time
to rest on well-placed benches.

We are walking as fast as we can
to stay alive as long as we can.

She pushed me in my stroller
around the block
and sang lullabies.
When my hand could reach for hers,
she told me stories I could not comprehend
of bad people
who took my grandparents away.
Later, we jogged side by side
and discussed a new war
and a world again gone mad.

We are still debating current affairs
as we exit the park,
her mind as agile as ever,
but now she worries
about a world she knows
she will never see
and I for one
I will ponder alone
while resting on a park bench.

Mike Frenkel
Fresh Meadows, New York

About "The Widening Gyre": A *Plainsongs* Award Poem

"The Second Coming" by William Butler Yeats might be the most important poem written in the last 100 years. Yeats' poem is often quoted and cited as representative of how modern society has come apart. In Mike Frenkel's "The Widening Gyre," the poet poses how people stay connected.

The poem is set in a park with walking paths where a man and his elderly mother take separate paths around the lake. The speaker mentions he walks "along the outer track, / six times around. / She takes the inner path / once around the lake." The mother's determination is shown to us as "She is hunched over, / leans heavily on her walker" where she "stops from time to time / to rest on well-placed park benches."

Frenkel's graceful lines and imagery present an understated power that achieves superb little gems throughout the poem: "We are walking as fast as we can / to stay alive as long as we can." Followed by: "She pushed me in my stroller / around the block / and sang lullabies." The related actions from the past to the present display connections of the relationship but also the larger cyclical nature of all relationships.

In another moment, we learn the mother had told the son "of bad people / who took my grandparents away." Then the current "new war / and world again gone mad." Reality includes hardships, and hardships create deep bonds. The combining actions of circling, history, and discussion appeal to our sense of struggle and determination. Frenkel does not take these qualities for granted and embraces what his mother has shown him about the world.

As the mother and son "exit the park" // she worries / about a world she knows / she will never see." The speaker leaves us with the eventual fact that he "will ponder alone / while resting on a park bench."

Michael Catherwood
Omaha, Nebraska

Coal Delivery Day, 1950

1.
Sunlight shuns
their dirt-floored cellar.
Red glow in its coal-hole
dwindles to embers
inside a cast iron
potbellied behemoth.
The coal man is on his way—
his thundering dump truck
eases down a snow-packed driveway
to a cellar window
this driver knows by heart.
He opens the truck's hatch,
clamps on a beat-up chute
and feeds it into the gap.
Black chunks
avalanche down the shaft
into a near-empty bin,
shepherded by the shovel-wielding father—
protective sentry in ash-coated coveralls—
scrupulous spreader
with pride in his heaped mound
of faceted firebringers
he kindles   pokes   stokes
coaxes a wavery flicker
into house-warming flames.

2.
Washday morning
the mother fills wicker baskets
with wet laundry
sloshed, wrung and rescued
from her coal-dusted Maytag.
She climbs from the cellar,
slides through January snow,
crunches underfoot
crushed remnants of summer lavender
and strewn coal—eyes and buttons

of melted snowmen.
She pulls a wet rag from her clothespin bag
and hand over head she trudges
up and down rows of wire clotheslines,
wipes them clean of settled soot—
and hangs sheets and starched schooldresses
to dry stiff and frozen in weak winter light.

3.
Drowsy girl roused from eiderdown
by whiffs of foul fumes
and the crash of tumbling nuggets
rubs her eyes and pads down cellar stairs
to roost on the bottom step
and watch her father
foster fresh flames.
She tiptoes back upstairs
to crouch over a cast-iron
floor grate. She squabbles
with her brother, shoves him
and claims the grate.
Fresh heat rises,
warms her flanks and balloons
her flannel nightgown.
She is Queen of the hot-air register.
Will she ever again feel so warm?

Elizabeth Stoessl
Portland, Oregon

About "Coal Delivery Day, 1950":
A *Plainsongs* Award Poem

The key to an effective long poem is to develop a structure that provides continuity. A reader needs to be able to move through the poem, holding on to what is being said as well as wanting to go further.

I very much like the structure of "Coal Delivery Day, 1950." Creating three stanzas works for the focus of the poem, laying out each segment with clear, direct language. The poet has developed what Marianne Moore called "a place for the genuine," rather than one that has "become so derivative as to become unintelligible."

Stanza 1 focuses on male-directed chores: the coal man driving his truck to deliver and unload coal at a location that he "knows by heart." The owner, the "shovel-wielding father," is almost a God-like figure who shepherds the coal, spreading it in the cellar and developing the fire.

Stanza 2 focuses on the female chore of washday as "the mother fills wicker baskets / with wet laundry / sloshed, wrung and rescued" and leaves the cellar to hang clothing on an outdoor line where the items will "dry stiff and frozen in weak winter light." The image of the frozen clothing contrasts well with the fire that is central to Stanza 1 and is prominent again in Stanza 3.

Stanza 3 focuses on the child who awakens to the sound of the coal delivery and then "pads down cellar stairs / to roost on the bottom step / and watch her father / foster fresh flames." She moves back upstairs "to crouch over a cast-iron / floor grate" where "[f]resh heat rises, warms her flanks and balloons / her flannel nightgown." This stanza incorporates both the visual aspect of her father as the master of the fire, as well as develops the image of her expanding nightgown in contrast to the frozen clothes that her mother pinned on the line.

The alliteration of this poem is incredible. The manner in which it captures this everyday occurrence of 1950 is both well depicted and visually appealing.

Becky Faber
Lincoln, Nebraska

The Forgotten War

In the snow a trail of boot prints
emerges from our wooded valley,
darkens the field up to our porch.
My father has returned from the silence
of the war once again. The war rages
deep among the trees and shadows,
and now he shutters himself in the house.
Fifty years since the war was over,
but this is how he brings it home with him:
in the bone settling silence of winter,
the dusting of snow, the frigid wind,
tire ruts half frozen, faint sweetness
of raw engine exhaust and burning wood.
Across the valley an old tree cracks
from the weight of snow. The report echoes.
Birds swoop from stark branches, descend
to where his boots exposed the black earth.

John Struloeff
Calabasas, California

Golem

I don't like the word you've carved
on my forehead. The last one still burns.
The next will, too. None of them animate me.

What makes me move is love, the scent
of violets, dances to join, stories to make.
the warmth of bread or sunshine.

I don't want the ovens of your rage,
don't want to harden into your fear,
or pain, or target. I'm not glazed. I'm leaving.

As I climb hills, my legs loosen
and my toes grip kindly rock. The wind
blows into my lungs. A kiss. A breath.

Mary Ann Dimand
Arvada, Colorado

Cultural Confusions

A deserted diner off the highway;
watched by the dark-haired, heavy waitress
I ate alone and uncomfortable.
Something wrong with her right eye
so craning round to see me better with the left.
Her Nebraska vowels offered pie Alamo-ed,
or so it sounded to my English ear.
After we sorted that out
she returned to lean and watch.
The coffee I ordered she placed down hard,
bending over me to ask, "Do you scream?"

Somewhere behind my ears splayed images
of weary torturers in Russian cellars,
racks, blades, pointed metal, Vlad, and Torquemada.
But here chainsaws for American carnage
in some slaughterhouse behind the kitchen.
Fight or flight, in turmoil to evade her half-closed eye.
Awareness seeping through my rising panic
of a small jug by my cup and
hearing the Nebraskan, 'Do you use cream?'

The sagebrush grasslands outside the window
have known more brutal cultural confusion.
I can see red hills in the distance,
the scratched line of a road, some cultivated land,
other scars that might be fences,
where Red Cloud had imagined it
stretching unboundaried for ever.

Kieran Egan
Vancouver, British Columbia, Canada

Stowaway

You sneak in beneath notice, thunder
down the runway, and are lifted
into crystalline air, much colder
than you imagined, the oxygen sucked
from your lungs. Here, you have lost
all landmarks, no more Mount Kenya,
even the color of your skin, blue with frost.
Your grip loosens, and—brief hysteria—
like Icarus, you are falling. Death, it seems,
is a kind of flight. Portentous as a meteor,
you enter a London yard where a sunbather dreams,
unready for the urgency he's about to encounter.
For a short while, you escaped borders and saw
the curve of the earth from above, unflawed.

Devon Balwit
Portland, Oregon

Grasslands

Let it be about farmed fields
corn tall and wheat flaxen.
The edges of town fenced—
planted into mowed lawns.

Sometimes it's about the plains.
Great Plains and high plains—vast
virgin prairies and, short grass
prairies, grasses for grazing.

You know it all—the whistle
of wind through seed heads.
A whiff of sage in the air from
nowhere. Sometimes it's a deep

tangle of roots far below ground
or a thatch of sturdy stalks
crisp underfoot—revealing
what you didn't see yesterday.

Then let it be about grasslands
unfenced—wide as the dome of sky
corralled by earth's curving. Then
we see everything and nothing.

Bonnie Larson Staiger
Bismarck, North Dakota

Keys

More than the art deco tables,
    the zebra print chairs,
the lamps shaped like stage lights,

    I come to the antique shop week
after week for the old keys. Tucked away in
    a cardboard box, rusted

and misshapen, of no use anymore.
    Most customers ignore them
or brush them off as junk.

    But in each key, I see an untold story,
a small part of me: my wariness
    in a blunted bit, my hesitance

in the dip of a collar—
    the metal piece just after
the stem and before

    the throat. This is also
where my secrets lodge—
    in the soft folds of my larynx.

Tenderly wrought
    histories in each scrape and groove.
Each move in and out, out and in

    of a lock wielded by frustrated, loving,
angry, impatient hands.
    But me: I always take my time.

I place each key in the center
    of my palm as if searching
for the perfect fit to unlock

    facets of myself I've been too afraid
or too hurried to recognize.
    Once, I put a key up to the store window

to let a tunnel of light shine
    through. The wave-like indentations
of the bow transformed

    the outside world into a sea.
All around me salt and algae.
    Key, from the Spanish *cayo*, meaning shoal or reef.

And suddenly, I was swimming
    with the woman next to me who had
once lent me her books. As she did, her sleeve

    slipped, revealing a pond-shaped birthmark
on her wrist. *No, it's an estuary.* In the water, her cap bobbed up
    and down like a sparrow against the sky.

If I had been braver, I would have loved
    her.
    I would have whispered to her:
take my hand and swim with me farther and
    farther

    past the sandbar. Let me hold you.
Let's take our time. Let's let every movement be
    outlined by metal and air. Our every turn.

                              Shannon K. Winston
                              Princeton, New Jersey

Eve Reflects

God, was I glad to get out.
You can't imagine how it was,
to look down at your own body
and time and again fail
to understand it.
One bite and I knew
I was all curves and crannies.
He knew it too,
by the look of his eyes.

After that we had to find hiding places.
We had to be discreet.
So we fell down among the shrubbery
and had our earthy fun
until the boss told us to take it outside.

And it's colder out here,
for sure,
but that's the worst of it.
Just means we spend more time
twined in our serpentine routine:
him up there
playing to the applause in his head;
me down in the shadows,
my head turned toward all the shrubs
whose names I now know.

Cecilia Gigliotti
Berlin, Germany

Storm Flow

Soot-gray tributaries creep over ridge
crests, offshoots of clouds that flood tree tops,
currents born from collisions of trapped cold
and fugitive heat, roiled through the sky
from south Alabama to east Tennessee — ocean,
creek, lake charmed to vapor, then gathered
together by chill to float above mountain
and plain, no longer land-locked, freed
from the paths of least resistance. Each drop
sails on wind, swells until Earth's slow gyre
compels them shimmering downwards,
water to sate root and trunk, to shine branches
once bent under this river's dark touch.

Robert Lee Kendrick
Clemson, South Carolina

Dirty Laundry

After Bethany Hays Erratic1_Watercolor and Tracy Truels' photo

So you found a stop sign ruptured
with bullet holes
Not a clean shot, as they say, holes too tight
to let in the sky, no matter how big that sky is, in Oklahoma.

I understand. Here in Portland, fire season looms,
and we are haunted by last year's ash,
coating the patio furniture like snow,
or no, draping the patio furniture like the comforter
I wore as a child, a homespun ghost,
those fraught mornings I hardly remember,
floating through the silences
in my parents' collapsing marriage.

Some people plant roses on the side of a highway.
This is something I know.

Years back, your husband, the nice guy,
painter of sea horses and namer of dogs,
punched a hole clean through a wall.
You drove to Mother Bear's,
and crouched in a wooden booth.
After eating, you swiped
a shimmer of gloss across your lips to seal them.

I mean to say, you must remember.

Did I tell you they used a nuclear bomb
to study the effect of radiation on rabbit corneas?
Put those rabbits right up at the test site, only
focused on the one thing, the rabbit eyes,
forest for the trees, and all. Of course
the bomb disintegrated, as they do,
the eyeballs and organs and every rabbit gesture
(every piece of flammable everything)
that could possibly be considered a specimen.

Remember that square in the middle of the country
where your dog liked you?

It's enough, really, to unravel the perforated line
of dance steps. To hold a blanket so grey it swells
like a storm cloud threatening to break or a dog
springing into your arms, convulsing.
Yet we don't. We dream of ocean trenches
And we lay down inside the origami of our anger.
Or we punch through our brutal need,
into every surface, breaking open the very first thing
we see that doesn't have a face.

Megan Savage
Portland, Oregon

The Lament of the First Chinese Brother

For you I swallowed the sea,
sucked in kelp, eels, tortoises, whales…
I held this in, so you could play
around the spiny crevices
carved by water and salt.

I watched you run, legs sleek
in the distance. Too far for me to see
more than your black hair shine, too far
to see if your hands cradled a starfish
or stroked the slick cushion
of the sand. Did you see

how hard I tried? How my cheeks tightened?
How my every movement
called out to you? How I knew
there was only so much sea I could hold?

Lisa Shirley
Yonkers, New York

A Martini Over a Stone Floor

At dawn, the desert hums.

The path covered in dirt.
Pebbles scattered
    under
        dry desert mesquite.

A bull's skull ornamentally hung

    over an open doorway.
    Bleached bones white. It is difficult.
    Ask

any mujer who has found herself degraded
into the puta of his life

on a bed over a stone floor.

Sometimes it gets bad.

Since learning this,
I've needed to sleep
two hours
each afternoon.

Often, I wake

tangled in shadow,

disoriented, angry, ranting, needing a vodka martini.

Adela Najarro
Capitola, California

The Map of the States

Hot asphalt. Heavy wool uniforms.
Plastic spats. The whole band
matched steps to painted stripes

on a street by the park. I still
feel sweaty when I try to speak.
How I reply in my softest voice—

I feared the dark park, men
on the street, long lean shadows
under my bed. I let my hair

down over my eyes. Held onto
my skirts as the wind swept
round the corner. Violet light

in a doctor's cold treatment room
suffused my rashes and blisters.
There are no more dime stores,

no days transparent as pages
of mica. No heavy black
phones that ring in the night.

It's still my country. Skin
close. Shaped as it was when
I opened my schoolbook

to the map of the states, their
starred capitals, all those places
I didn't know I'd be going to.

Barbara Daniels
Sicklerville, New Jersey

Leaving the Concert Hall

She is eleven, maybe twelve,
but numbers no longer matter,
for she has heard Bach and Mozart
for the first time,
has mastered the mathematics of the wind,
the heart's algebra,
where A is not A and need not be,
and now her fingers conduct the weather
until it shivers with illuminations.

She walks, then skips, then
spins to a private pantomime
that need not reveal itself,
for she is the conductor.
Silent notes come swirling round her
in wizard colors of the new,
and the ecstatic leaves whirl
in xylophones of dance.
She feels her joy float from breath to breath.

Bezeled light dazzles round a point,
a perfect jewel, emerald, topaz, diamond,
and everything is all right, for a moment all right.
Then, as the sky imagines a storm,
and the school bus pulls up,
she folds a crescendo inside a breeze,
and sets it free.

Sean Lause
Bluffton, Ohio

Andromeda

They only ask girls to sacrifice themselves
only chain virgins to rocks. If they were to ask
a grown woman, worn down by children
already tiring of life,
already used to settling for less than the stuff of her dreams
it wouldn't really be a sacrifice.
It would just be one more unpleasant chore
something to get through during the course of a day.
"Of course I'll do it," that tired woman would say.
"Just let me finish up here and I'll be right out."

Monsters mean different things
to girls and women. For one
there's the terrifying possibility of being devoured
physically or spiritually, the end of great plans
great dreams. For the other, the chance to meet a monster
is a break from monotony, the happy realization
that the unexpected does still exist outside
the four walls of a day.

Holly Day
Minneapolis, Minnesota

Requiem, Father

Finally now I can see you,
after being blinded by your power

from the spring morning we raced in the yard
when you loped big and easy ahead of my striving

until the night in the cold room where you were gone
from the form on the table,

until tonight when
those are your eyes in the mirror,

tonight when my son was the way
I must have been so many times—

home again but with traveling
in his eyes, with the vision he follows

not letting him see here, now,
or that someday he might have these eyes.

C. E. Greer
Wellington, Colorado

100 Blessings

With cactus, everything moves in slow motion.
The slow turning of the grizzly bear prickly pear
towards sun; its painstaking,

persistent sinking of roots—
deep and deeper, divining dampness
secreted from sunlight, from drought.

Still, distress yellows it, withers it.
I push four stakes deep into porous, poor soil,
uprighting four succulent stems.

My thanks are needles embedded
in my fingers and sweatshirt, irksome
as spidery threads of fiberglass.

I pick at them, wipe and wipe again,
transferring ethereal shards of harassment
back and forth that stick and stick again.

If there is fortune in dream
or misfortune in nightmare,
I have neither and instead,

tap the drizzle of memory
or image's clammy dampness
unearthing grace in the creaking

ache of revelation, realizing
that some things are unable or unwilling
to be summed up.

I wait for the shock of bright yellow
blossoms spreading open for the sun;
the ripening fruit—

watery-sweet and packed tight
with seeds, like a hundred blessings
needing to begin.

Alan Toltzis
Yardley, Pennsylvania

Unknown Elegy

Pasolini was an atheist
with a nostalgia for belief.
When the police found his blood
in the wheel well of an Alfa Romeo,
it was a *giallo* film.

A girl from my hometown vanished
and we all hoped she just ran off with her boyfriend.
She took her cell phone with her
for Chrissakes.
They found her body three days later
in a warehouse full of road salt.

Driving along Highway 1,
the fog is so thick
I wish fireflies would appear
like that summer as a kid
I stayed at my father's house.
"Come take a ride with me," the man said.
"I'll give you a present."

They say one day we'll meet again.
I think about that sometimes.

Will Simescu
Fort Collins, Colorado

Moths

Dance through a spiral fracture of porch light,
ballet the leaded glass, their slippered feet
feeling about for purchase against the night.

I fear them, symbols of death and rebirth,
just like Christ and the seasons. Anything
with no mouth that eats can't be right.

I wish they were still slugs, fetid
crawling creatures hidden deep underfoot,
that blind sphere down there at the base

chain of being. No true moth flutters
that did not once feed upon a corpse.
I am certain of this. Look at their eyes,

swirling nihilistic gyres, nothingness pooling out
like the infinite rings of collapsing stars.
They would fly into your mouth. No hesitation,

just a fatal gust and then—*God!*—mayhem between your teeth.
I want them to stop haunting our house,
but summer is long, and the light remains

bright over our door deep into the P.M.
when I hear them wisping the glass,
tickling burned sand with hairs that pass for feet

as I sink to sleep in the huddled dark.
Don't want to wake the baby. Don't
want to know what spirits dance outside,

waving wings through the black.

C.M. Barnes
Denver, Colorado

Taking Down the Clothes

Unpinning her way into the winded
backs of shirts, my mother
takes down laundry, the flailing
legs and bleached arms, too, reaching
out or collapsing, ungainly
as first love; and me, backing
onto the grass close
enough to see bottoms
up, drunken trousers swaying
in place, crinolines naive
enough to lift with any puff
of wind, and mother tossing
aside wrists and cuffs and taking
that bunch down.
So many clothespins
arcing toward the rusted
tin I hold as a childhood
game, and my company
of escapees, their heads,
their legs like mine,
but made for holding on.

Anne Knowles
Valencia, California

Our Daughter in Darkness

Our daughter, latter day Persephone,
has slipped chthonic into a darkness
we can not penetrate, can not visit.
There, she says she dines on the dark ruby
seeds, the dried blood seeds, the pomegranate
that's her own split flesh, her own magic seeds,
but we think it's the poppy seed she ingests,
that milky nectar that holds her, that keeps
her quiet in her world of twilight and shade.
She emerges from time to time to bring
us tears, to moisten our nest with weeping,
to re-tell her sad tale of abduction,
to lament her losses and what she has become,
but never stays long in our blinding land,
where she says both light and air are toxic.

Cecil Morris
Roseville, California

Circle Dance

Festival Circle Dance led
by eighty-two-year-old Ponca
elder slowly and carefully

makes his way round a sun-
drenched, mowed herb patch,
like a tortoise racing against

time. Native leader presents
him a star quilt crowned
with an eagle for his service

to country and tribe
like the rock star he is
to them. Young dancers,

shake hands, thank him,
a Korean War Air Force veteran,
for teaching them dance

meanings, how to make
regalia, moccasins, and for
keeping his culture alive.

He tells of surviving heart attack,
mourning loss of his wife,
dead thirteen years,

harder than going to war.
We step forward, clumsily
trail fringed blankets,

and jingle bell shirts
around circle, doing our best
to follow his lead.

Lin Marshall Brummels
Winside, Nebraska

The Fundamentals

Those minerals erupting
from maxillae and mandibles

show our roots to the hard
earth that will not yield

to soft circumstance if it
can manage—like these choppers

and mashers above and under
food for more than just thought

that often bites back
with acid or crunch

etching the enamel
or cracking the crown

so requiring repair
to those bone-cousins

of calcium and other rocky
concerns not so resilient

as these cakes and crackers
springing back into the maw

as they must if the mouth and
all behind maintain that line,

bowstring-taut to that bedrock
from which ridge and flesh burst.

John Zedolik
Pittsburgh, Pennsylvania

Dirt Time

It comes on like a hunger, visceral
and not to be denied. It is in the nose,
the tongue, but mostly in the legs and back,
aching to get close again, to bend and touch
and go under. Into the subterranean,
hands and shovel and trowel burrowing
like a gopher, nose twitching as the smells
of worms, minerals, the dead and newly living,
are released. Sweat beads on forehead, drips down chest,
stains back. Silt, sand, clay, loam. Easy and yielding.
Root thick. Sticking like glue. Rich and heavy.
Dig deep, into and through. Lift the load upward,
and toss it off, hips swiveling, abdomen
tightening, the machinery in fine tune. I
say there is nothing better than making
a hole and planting, tamping down the earth
softly like putting a child to bed, letting
the water slowly filter down to the roots
you've separated, like you do to a lover's
hair falling over her face, to find that mouth,
that peace and passion. The sun burns your back,
the day is smeared on your face, tattoos arms, lays
a coat of dust on pants, cakes boots. Mud and
water and light we are. I dig myself and fill the hole.

**Robert Rothman
San Francisco, California**

How Much Does the Anne Frank House Cost?

You wrote hope
in the one book you could lock,
mapping first the layout of the annex;
inventorying the rooms' details:
Linoleum, mahogany chairs, the stockroom's cinnamon, cloves, and
    peppers ground, the Delft
toilet, laboratory sink…
To the walls
you turned, underneath the tacked-up celluloid smiles
—Ginger Rogers, Rudy Vallee, Princess Juliana—
doodles marking hours
spent sniffing at the windowsill,

that rat-crack listening for gulls and bells,
the Westertoren bells, their music maybe
melted down for *Die Wehrmacht.*

But the bookcase, the bookcase,
a wall of words
—atlases, catalogues, account ledgers—
kept the footfalls back, the eyes averted
until it finished your sentence.

Now everybody knows this address.

"How much does the Anne Frank house cost?"
they all ask now,
wanting mostly to get out of it.

What if
you walked
out from under this poem?
Made a left on Prisengracht along the sunlit canal,
easy past cafes, aroma of cigars and licorice chocolates,
kept going under the chestnuts toward Nieuwe Spiegelstraat,
onto green Vondelpark,
and then off the map
where the Westertoren bells can't be heard

and what if, this poem, begun by a wall of words,
had no ending

Sharon Kennedy-Nolle
Bedford, New York

Hoax

There's a child in a cage
who knows just one word:
mama she screams

ah here's a shot
to calm her no
we cannot have that
noise and misbehavior
keep them quiet so
they will disappear
under a searing sun
and a noncommittal moon
and they are brown
and in rags and
her mama
ran with her
under one arm
days and nights
in a desert full of animals
and stars cradled
in her mother's embrace
sturdy as the red rocks
brave as cacti
that thrive without water
please please refugees
they smell of sweat
and thirst they have
forgotten the hunger
whose reedy voice
echoes under the ribs
the child is shoved in this line
the woman in another

but you imagine this
all propaganda
some people are not
people some are not even

people they are not like us
they are not

fake news

**Donna Pucciani
Wheaton, Illinois**

Palmyra, Illinois

We loaded up the minivan at four
and drove the twenty minutes north from home
through uniform and silent corn and soybeans.
It's just a clearing in the corn, the town
that raised my father. Now it houses only
a stubborn seven hundred, those who lack
my dad's good sense or never had a chance
to leave. Palmyra looks like one of those
elderly men whose bodies shrink as years
go by. Their skin remains the same, as if
remembering their carnal maximum.
Empty and lifeless streets, exclusively
north-south, east-west, this being Illinois,
brought us to Dad's old house, his childhood home.
Dad cleared his throat, as if to start a story.
He didn't, and we drove back home in silence.

Jared M. Campbell
New York, New York

tortoise

all afternoon we searched for you,
amidst floridian cacti and palm fronds,
tall grass and trees.

when i finally spotted you, i called to my brothers.
you were small, faster perhaps
than we expected, afraid.

it is alright, tortoise,
to be small and afraid,
large shadows over you threatening
one collapse or another.

now, a hundred miles away,
months later and months of snow
and other storms to come,
i dream of you.

i, too, am small, afraid
to peek my head out of my shell,
my blissful ignorance, my hiding place.

who knows if the shadows
are friend or foe?
we will have to wait,
poke out our tender faces,
and see.

Genevieve Hartman
Rochester, New York

The White Season

The petals crack upon the plot
    the flowers dying there
        the white season ain't forgiving
The warmer weather long-forgot
    the autumnal nightmare
    spring's nakedness laid bare
    for the lecherous to stare
        some old graves ignore the living
        in the cold, the dead ain't shiv'rin'

The writer fumbles with the plot
    the hero isn't there
        the white season's hair is thinning
Some ends are marked by little blots
    some writ in ink and some are not
    some souls inspire and some are bought
    it happens everywhere
    when the heart's no longer there
    it's making myths that we despair
        the white season's for the living
        from the end to the beginning

The frost creeps in upon the plot
    the bones grow frozen fare
        the white season is rebuilding
And freezing water stops the rot
    the bones no longer care
    the heart's no longer there
    the soul goes anywhere
        a white season goes on living
        from the end to the beginning

Miguel Eichelberger
Vancouver, British Columbia, Canada

For Samuel Morse

The enemy was distance
and you conquered it.
Bravo! Congratulations!

Now your dots and dashes
are the zeros and ones
driving computers and cellphones.

Now we cannot escape one another.
Everywhere is here.
Anytime is now.

And all are lost in information,
washed by a river of unrelated facts,
besieged by a thousand claims.

And who can listen?
Who has the time?
Bravo! Congratulations!

It all reminds of Thoreau's comment
when he learned of your wonderful invention:
But suppose the person in New Jersey
who can now talk with a person in Texas
has nothing important to say.

Mark Christhilf
Nutley, New Jersey

Self-portrait with Memory

Annoyingly, she is a younger *she*,
standing too close to your creaking
shoulders and bad knees, too close
to your almost-deaf ear where she talks
too loudly for too long about people and places
you can't remember from far away; too close
to the crow's-feet around your eyes; too close
to red-veined spiders trekking across thighs,
to age spots multiplying on the backs of hands
that try to swat her away, then—suddenly—for the love
of Memory, draw her too close—or not close enough—right here
beside your forgetful heart, beside all your automated
rhythms of open, close; open, close.

Marjorie Maddox
Williamsport, Pennsylvania

Hailstorm Disquiet

What renders you more vulnerable
than waiting at a stoplight
in a hailstorm, hail pebbles pouncing
and bouncing everywhere,
threatening your windshield,
denting your car? Who stands still
in a hailstorm anyway? Even
laying hens scuttle off to their coop.
But there you are,
    stranded,
held back by an unwavering,
glaring red traffic signal,
letting marbles and golf balls—
surely a dozen for every wrong
you have ever committed—
pound like buckshot
out of a surly black sky.
And the light still red,
    red
as a proud Gala apple
with no intention of
turning green.

Marilyn Dorf
Lincoln, Nebraska

White Buffalo Woman

—for Hollis

You told me to wear something
beyond me to your daughter's party—
the one you raised by yourself
for thirteen years—so I came in
this sweater with its vaguely
Lakota-like designs
and you were ecstatic to see
me in fertile red shapes set so purposefully
against thirsting ochers
and mute bands of sand.

Later, in the dim light
of my small apartment,
the narrow hallway closing
back in around me,
I find the small white plume
sticking to my sweater at the center
of my ribs
close to where the heart
might be—just a feather
from my own down coat—
but now I believe the
bit of down must
have come from being near
your spirit—the same
that laid the array of feathers
around the leather figurine
of the White Buffalo Woman
that stands on your end table,
her bow drawn taut
to assure me
there are other imaginable horizons
in the direction of her aim.

Wyle McClain
Ridgefield, Connecticut

They Say of Rain

They say it comes down in sheets.
And just so I saw it and
heard the rain hard on the roof,
as if it were the thunder of hooves
only prairie grasses heard
before the buffalo were gone.

The sheets of rain I saw were grey,
as if they were bedsheets
soiled and washed too many times.
Perhaps in the old ways:
by hand across a washboard
or in the river and beaten upon rock.

If you fell asleep in them, the smell
of rain would cleanse
your nightmares from memory
and you would only remember the heroic
dreams or dreams of feisty love.

The rain went on longer—much longer
than the evening news—
and so it kept me from the trivial and tragic.

When it stopped,
it was not all of a sudden, so as to surprise,
but gradually—lowering in intensity,
like agreement after argument.
Or hearing a child crying herself to sleep.

Perhaps it took as long as for buffalo
trampled grass to lift up the morning dew.

Chet Corey
Bloomington, Minnesota

Forecast

As I peruse websites,
a photo of bloated feet
pops up captioned
with "4 signs you are
about to die
of a heart attack."
The feet, attached
to hairy swollen legs,
are as swollen as mine.
I have packed newborn
clothes into the hospital bag
and listened to birthing
affirmations. I swam
one mile last night,
and my feet shrunk
to their regular size.
But when I woke,
they looked like skin
balloons again. All day,
the forecast has predicted
rain, but clouds are still
pregnant, and swallows
swarm trees and power lines,
eating mosquitoes
and looking like bats.

Francine Rubin
Arlington, Massachusetts

Ghost Leg

To be here, I've gone back
to find what I tore from myself.

Then and now,
we survivors do what we must,
finding only later
our willingness to snap the bone
has lost its savor, is not
as clean a break as we believed.

The teeth of love biting deeper
its need holding fast.

Joseph Hardy
Nashville, Tennessee

History Lessons

I remember I thought it was too poignant to be true the way sometimes you look up from the table and I swear the tone turns sepia or black and white anyway with a tenderness I only ever saw in films at the rep cinema before it shut down for good—it was that part in the history book about Russian soldiers in the First World War dying prostrate in the mire while they scribbled pictures of the Virgin on scraps of paper, bobbing up and down (the writer said) like exotics, their heads wreathed in bright flame, the sky behind them spattered in gold leaf combustibles. I went looking for the entry to read to you but could not find it so just trust me when I tell you and did you know they say that mustard gas smells for all the world like lilac and harvest?

Christopher Snook
Dartmouth, Nova Scotia, Canada

Friends

I can be your friend. Trust me.
Whatever the true story I tell,
you can and you will top it.
Thus do I become your buddy.

If I had foot blisters in Paris,
you had a bout of peritonitis
in an over-populated hostel
somewhere in Paraguay.

My dad, a Marine, weathered
boot camp at Parris Island.
Your granderdad was a Ranger;
bayonetted several Krauts.

My tales are grounded,
state-side company clerks.
Yours come in from above,
paratroopers risking it all.

I could say, "Go ahead.
Give me a story, any story,
and I will bottom it."
But it's always my turn first.

All I can say is
I have never told
an untopped story.

And I have more friends
than anyone in the world.

Mark Metcalf
Sutton, Nebraska

LIFE and Ruby Bridges

January 22, 2019
We stand in front
of self-checkout
buying pads and my love
picks up a magazine and cries
*How are they going to do a cover about the 60s with no Black people
   on it?*

White faces stare at us:
customers in the store—this state
is full of white faces—and images
on the page—JFK, NASA,
The Beatles, and a caption:
The decade when everything changed.

I stare
at those words
I read them out
loud—oh, the white faces
around the store, around those words
LIFE. I'll remember that.

The magazine goes back
on the shelf and we pay
for our pads and we walk
to the exit,
faces like *LIFE*, still
stare and my love says
I'm making the white people uncomfortable.
And I say
Good.

January 23, 2019
I stand in front
of a little girl, trying
to meet her eyes, and recall
LIFE. The Problem We All Live With.

I look at the little girl—
between grown men with no faces,
every fist clenched
except bloody hands that can't be washed—
clean socks tucked into clean little shoes,
hair pulled back
clean, dress
clean, skin
clean, yet unwashed

*How are they going to do a cover about the 60s with no Black people
    on it?*
The decade when everything changed.
The Problem We All Live With.
I see—
on the leaking blood
on the cover of *LIFE*
at the expressions in the checkout line—
the writing on the wall.

Calida Osti
West Lafayette, Indiana

Acroyoga

Flex your trust muscle, the instructor advises,
making us giggle. Practicing the poses,
my sister and I alternate being flyer or base.
Now, my back flat on the mat, our hands clasped,
wrists stacked, cores contracted, my feet
supporting her thighs, she leans over me.
I straighten my legs to ninety degrees,
lofting her toward the spring sky,
an acrobat of strength and grace. Her blue eyes
mirror mine, assuring me,
she will always be my spotter—
each capable of bearing a sister's weight.
Once captive, we have survived grief's hot center,
our wings sturdier than wax and feather.

Janis Harrington
Chapel Hill, North Carolina

Open

I want to spill open with you.
Start here. Find some fissure and split

me open simply with your silver hammer.
I want you to open me.

This is how I come to you
obsidian, black gem.

It's not about the color
of the moon.

Tap. Tap here.
Tap. Spill me open

so we can see, together, if there is
sand or more rock inside.

I do want you to know me
for who I am really.

It is because of our difference
black to white, fire to water

straight to trans, Muslim to agnostic
that I want to get to know you

through the things you do to me
and the things you let me do to you.

Let's crack past crystalline layers
to bits of sediment, sand, gold.

One day we will marvel at the way you split me open
and how you let me reach inside of you

past your armor to the things you were
not sure you held inside of you.

Rachel Tramonte
Cleveland Heights, Ohio

Sun Salutation

My mother was made of sun:
Corona of strawberry-blonde rays
Around a celestial-body face.
At dawn she sang the curtains open,
"Let the sunshine in!"

Baby oiled skin, bikini slung low
On the dock at the lake
Or clasped in ultraviolet lamps
Seeking warmth.

Not long she reigned
Queen of adult swim
Teenage muscle memories
Guarding lives as sunburn blisters
Shortened her own.

My mother's cancer was made of sun:
Nuclei slashed by radiation
Skin occupied by malignant starlight
A total eclipse.

Someday the sun will die.
Fuel exhausted, core collapsed
A swelling planetary nebula
Blown by stellar wind
To begin life anew
Elsewhere.

Kara Mae Brown
Goleta, California

Poem for the Dog Jaya

Generous teacher,
I begin to fathom
what you've tried to convey,

about enthusiasm
how it opens each moment
to an ordinary radiance;

and how the wind speaks
the language of the trees
though it's much easier for you

living in a world without names
or only a single name
which is *world,*

every new face
divine enough
to deserve your love.

John Krumberger
Minneapolis, Minnesota

The New Particle

A matter-of-factness in the back
pages cannot be enough
when the ivory towers introduce
us to the new particle they say
had to be there, the nothing
that was doing something.
A heretofore undetected speck,
a mortar to our all inclusive dust;
it's implausible, must be a jest,
a card trick of the physicists.

It's too startling an utterance
so early, the sun barely up.
A serving of the indigestible—
how do we get it down, an account
of how things really stand?
I put butter to the toast
but go back to the paragraph
on the adhesive of constellations,
an infinitesimal hand tying knots.
They've made true the mad surmise

Of learned men, and some of us
want to understand the distillation
of science out of shadow play.
But how, in our tight diameters,
do we actually touch this news,
how address this maestro of the dark
matter that is almost everything?
How do we come by a fluency
in an undreamt-of common language?
I turn the page to conventional

considerations or the usual meteorology
after reading the little to be
said about the omnipresent.
Science has read its instruments
and announces now the new particle

that rivets even imperceptible suns,
prints the spinning grammar we inhabit,
invisibly making visible
the astounding cog it makes turn
as it otherwise would not.

Todd Johnson
Racine, Wisconsin

Water Ceremony

I'll collect a few ounces from all the bodies of water I love:
    Marsh Creek Reservoir
    Lake Winola
    the Susquehanna River
    a farm pond in Chester Springs
    White Fish Lake
I'll boil it all in a big pot,
let it cool, and chug every drop.
Maybe I'll chant a few words first.
Something solemn or reverent.
I'm curious about the change
that'll come over me, as it must.
Will my flesh transmogrify to fluid?
Will I track little puddles behind me?
Maybe I'll flow downhill toward the sea
where all my molecules will mingle with the world's waters
until I return to the land as rain.
I don't know how long I'll be gone
or if my friends and family will recognize me.

Michael Phillips
Exton, Pennsylvania

Staggering Bees

Flowers abandoned at the burial site.
The black car doors slam shut.

Guests shed their coats and express
sympathy, unforgiving of mortality.

Platters of cold cuts,
homemade salads, store-bought buns

and boxed desserts—but I do not
want them.

Women bring more food: a bowl of olives,
cheese and crackers, Jell-O with whipped cream topping.

Someone places her hand on my shoulder,
says: *be sure to get yourself*

a plate, dear. I turn away,
look out the window, and cross

my arms against the world.
It guides me toward the blooming lilacs

and staggering bees,
to the laughing voices of children

playing on the swing set
under the backdrop of clouds and sunbreaks.

All this.
Yet none of it.

Yvonne Higgins Leach
Vashon, Washington

Is Pluto Still a Planet?

Occasionally the darkness lumbers in.
Heavy clodhoppers stomp mud
Upon the clean tiles. One smashed violet
Clinging to its sole.

Winged maple seeds litter the drive like
Tolls paid by fallen angels. Stroll
In the oak savanna where cool shadows
Absolve the solemn codas of despair.

A hem of blackbirds on the wire.
A colony of cumulonimbus.
Prayer and good wishes offered after
Tragedy are gestures impotent as cut flowers
Whose fragrance fouls in a yellowed glass.

On the white balcony, you overlook
A canopy of leaves. Birdsong fills
The promise of late spring. A crow
In the sycamore. An album of the
Unidentified. The red canoe in the loft.
A stiffened saddle on a barn-peg.
The jaws of Japanese beetles.
This life, that is all you'll ever have.

Joan Colby
Elgin, Illinois

Abattoir

Slaughter occurs more perverse
in seeing what's coming,
hammer swinging, metal bolt
locking, unlocking in equal

destiny. Gutsy intestine returns
to dirt, bloody clods
mass produced to cellophane
standards. Fear turns, vile

names honor their disgraced
ideals and indexed dreams
burned and rendered. Dead
grease gone come morning.

He who waxes evening
floors shines his reflection
whenever pains of chest
or cheat look into

the face of what
he eats. These places
seek to shame death
into picking up the

check. These places demand
squeamish, farm-raised swine
bred organic, trading steroids
for self-medicating antibiotics.

Marc Meierkort
Glendale Heights, Illinois

Battle of Los Angeles, 2006

I have
spent

4
days (3 nights)
in Los Angeles

I flew there. 6
hours, cramped, to
watch
a trifecta of
shows in the rundown
recesses of Reseda.

I remember

walking the street from
the rent-a-car
to the sardine can-like VFW

avoiding

glass splintered in
the sidewalk
crushed
Buds and
crushed
butts thrown
from rusted pickups
on to trash
piles
set aside for
pickup.

Against a wall of
the building next
to the
VFW,
where the tournament

had
already begun,

leaned
    a
        stained,
            soiled,
                California King.

Across the parking lot, in front
of the VFW, in
plain view,
Steen and Sydal
worked
through the
mechanics of their
match.

They,
like L.A.,
were ruining
the illusion.

Eric Kennedy
Hastings, Nebraska

The Definition

For my grandfather, a Vietnam vet

When you were there, time was infinite
and silent, fragile, vivid and bright.
War connected that matrix inside of you.

Coming home, you could tell time
by the sun's very arch, knew light from
preordination. You knew
what corners held IEDs,
what edges to avoid, when to stop.

But when the sun sinks below
the parched horizon,
you have no reference point,
only stars overhead.
They burn dead light,
pushing past a billion black holes
to reach us, just now, millenniums away.

Jayne Warren
Norwood, Massachusetts

Sediment Remains

The bridge collapsed
as pilgrims crossed and
snow settled over them
before the town square
tugged bricks into herringbone.

I order milky tea
and hear the quarrel of two lovers
across the square—

the fight is a series of I nevers,
some virtuous, some sorrowful
arms dangling over a balcony
in mock serenade,
one hand gripping a bottle of wine,
feet slipping on a rug,
the elusive & elastic tango,
chattering in the museum's night.

Samn Stockwell
Barre, Vermont

Footfall

Looking down the hillside
A mild, cool northerly breeze
Countering Spring's wet heat
Infinite space and endless possibilities
Flower upon flower
Blade upon blade
Gliding birds
Skipping butterflies

One foot forward, then the other
Striding down and ahead,
Faster and faster
Arms balancing the jostled movements
Some footfalls firm,
Thumping the hard ground,
Others press into the dirt with a sigh,
A knee bends, the hip turns
Maneuvering past bunched milkweed
Hopping over hollowed tree trunks
Dropping into patches of sunken earth
Breathing

Slowing but still moving
Approaching the bottom and its ancient story
Recited in layers of soil
Digging the depths of its knowledge
Searching for its lessons
Contemplating its age as days of sunlight,
Cycles of rain, generations of creatures
Searching for its meaning

Pleading for another chance to descend the hill,
Another opportunity to feel the warmth,
The moisture, the wind,
The confidence, the doubt,
Another opportunity to watch the birds,
The butterflies, the swaying milkweed,
Another life to contemplate beauty and fragility,

Existence and wonder,
Another chance to observe the bees hovering,
The beetles crawling beneath the log,
The centipede weaving around the tiny twigs
Embedded in the damp earth
That gave way beneath a quieter,
More subtle, more considered footfall

Christopher Goedert
Smith Center, Kansas

Lesson Learned

Naturally, I burst into tears.
No one had ever told me
one day I might tumble off the school bus,
wave goodbye to TJ,
and fling open my front door
to find no one home.
I stood clutching my Flintstones lunchbox.
Where was my mother?

Into the house's long, perfidious silence
a knock thundered.
No one had ever told me
not to answer the door when I was alone,
so I opened it.

Trumpet case in hand, Brian Shumway
stood on the front step, ready to practice
a beginner's version of "The Carnival of Venice"
with my sister at the piano.
"Nobody's here!" I blurted.
He gaped at my tear-streaked face,
then shuffled back to his mother's station wagon
purring at the curb.

Later my mother reproached me for crying.
I was a big girl now. I needed to show
some resourcefulness next time
I found myself alone.

A few weeks later a Chrysler glided up
beside the patch of dirt where TJ and I
were digging a parking garage
for our tiny plastic cars.
Lucille, my father's kind-faced secretary,
leaned toward the open passenger window
and said she'd been sent to fetch me.
My mother had been detained.
Placidly I replied I would be fine where I was

and kept digging. Astonished,
Lucille tried to coax me to come with her
but eventually drove back to the bank alone.

Everyone had forgotten
what they'd always told me:
never accept a ride
you haven't asked for.

Patricia L. Hamilton
Jackson, Tennessee

Hope

in the charred
far back corner
of the burned
blackened backlot
one green blade
of grass remains

Margo L. Foreman
Lincoln, Nebraska

Opportunity

From the ridge
Above the slippery grass of the creek bank,
We stare down at the carcass of the steer.
Late sun warms our backs,
Inks our silhouettes onto the opposite hill
As if we are the string of cut-out people in the frame
Above the sideboard in the ranch house.

Like our old black table upended
After a kitchen argument,
The steer, huge and hairy,
Rests on its back,
Wedged against a decaying tree trunk,
Legs as stiff and straight as posts,
Useless to leverage the enormous body.

Near the end of the tree trunk,
The head reveals no answers to our sympathetic speculation
Of the steer's final fall.
Detached and disconnected,
Angled unnaturally,
Neck eaten away to the green grass,
Face mutilated into mixed media art
Swirls of red and grey with teeth and hair.

Within the boundaries of the four legs,
Guts and bones lie torn, shredded,
Strewn like a bloody buffet,
Tossed by the coyotes
Who pulled in for a quick meal,
Beckoned by a pair of ribs,
Smooth, clean, and vaulted,
Rising high above the entrails
Like Golden Arches.
Fast food on the high plains.

We move on.

Maria Anderson Knudtson
Omaha, Nebraska

Sourgrass and Tadpoles

Things live where things would not seem:
Sourgrass as though it had rooted, nudged
Away some more civilized weed, or tadpoles
In mudholes, connected to no stream,
No parent fish or frog around, only the brown
Splashes of water left from Tuesday's rain
And the heat of a summer sun. On the edges
The yellow butterflies and the white, small,
Simple, a fit for this modest place where beauty
Can be one color, small, its elegance born
Of tiny miracles, like flight, or, better yet: life.

Robert Parham
Clarkesville, Georgia

My maiden aunts

composed on salvaged envelopes
cut open and laid flat to show
their pure insides (like fish
filleted by a letter opener);
a habit learned in the Depression
with the meager means that all endured.
For years they scavenged greeting cards
from which they cut the pictures
and the printed words to make
their patchwork palimpsests.
From a dozen cards might come
a single colored Christmas greeting
with a note, perhaps, handwritten on
the bottom or the back, to niece
or nephew who enjoyed the treat.

Ed Block
Greendale, Wisconsin

Stocking Shelves at Hills Supermarket—1974

An ideal summer job before grad school
    graveyard shift with pay differential
        (and days free for the beach)
    easy work remaking the store each night
    locked doors and no customers
    a boss more pal than boss
    progressive rock on the PA system.

I brown bagged my lunch
and, for 6 nights, my 2 co-workers
tempted me by eating
    chips, pop, desserts, donuts, deli meats, lobster
    37,00 sq. ft. of free food, they said.

I caved on the 7th night
    roast beef on a hard roll
    Coke and pretzels
    endless Sealtest Cherry Vanilla ice cream

For the rest of the summer
I was willingly complicit in gorging
on whatever the shelves offered
and beyond

    I organized menus
    took orders
    collected what we'd eat
    fashioned a paper *toque blanche*
    prepared our meals,
    tossed out the excesses of each night.

Extra benefit?
Employee store loss?
Wanton self-indulgence?
Pilfering?
Theft?

I knew all this and none of it mattered
until 6 months later when I read

>   *There was a ship, quoth he.*

Geo. Staley
Aloha, Oregon

Cashier Strays from Register

The Current River floods the mill
turned restaurant and tourist machine,
grinding out summer jobs and dollars
to forest families whose ancestors
homesteaded 40-acre patches
of Ozark rock. A rebuild delivers
new limestone and cedar to the riverbanks.
A long-time cashier siphons her lunch break
to churn her tired legs past construction buckets
to the river rocks. Against the stench
of stranded bluegills, a perfume.
She hobbles between crawdad carcasses
and wildflowers taking root
beside giant stones. Amid the grass-like
nobodies of nature's blooms,
a clump of Downy Phlox,
plump and lavender,
thick against her ankles
and fragrant in noontime sun.

Dave Malone
West Plains, Missouri

Sometime After My Father Died

I follow a creek through the woods.
Mud smacks, squelches, and suction-cups
to my boots. I come across a fallen tree,
clinging to the river bank. Its gnarled, serpent
roots dip and curl through the murky grass.
The spongey trunk sinks into the loose ground,
hoping the water washes it away before its tomb
swallows. Lowering myself, I lay my hands
on this fallen giant and admire bees alighting
on almost unfurled ferns, birds hopping
around its leaves, mushroom umbrellas drying
after the rain. I make sure to withhold hope.
I am not an answer to anybody's prayers, only another body
paying respects and resting on its limbs.
    Lying on its back, under thick, glistening
    patches of moss,
    dying, I can do nothing but watch,
    again.

Tate Lewis
Bloomington, Illinois

In the Air

(Originally published in The Magnolia Review)

Dispossessed
of ancient mysteries
we fly

above the clouds
they cast their shadow
as do you

a white wing
reaching out
to blue hills

a ripple of breeze
on the waters
the quivering thought

of whatever god is
carrying you off
in one fell swoop

into the unseen

in midair
amidst the laughter
of passengers

on their way
South   where
the birds have gone

for the winter
We'll look up
at those pelicans

and see your strong wings
your beak that carried food
for us   and would have

pierced your own breast
to feed us
in the early years

Later you learned
to protect yourself
your flight
into your own   delight

                                  Naomi Ruth Lowinsky
                                  Pleasant Hill, California

Secrets

At the lavishly spread table
the dinner party guests,
all writers
rehearse the usual subjects,
falling into the ancient and dangerous litany
of terrible childhoods—drunken fathers,
households in the grip of nutty religions,
various shades of poverty,
possible abuse.
I sit quietly.
And then, inevitably, crazy mothers
are marched out
which brings a competitive spirit,
a kind of survival pride.
I sit quietly.
our hostess says, we all have
difficult stories.
I sit quietly
Until my husband outs me—
except my wife, he says.
The others look at me skeptically,
unsure of my place in their communion.
I look penitent and apologetic,
My lovely childhood hanging on me
Like a curse.

Carol Bason
Santa Barbara, California

Nothing

Nothing exotic in the park today:
not the red tailed hawk mobbed
by a murder of maternal crows,
nor the golden eagle that swooped
for a squirrel and had us wheezing
in wonder and horror,
nor the fox I thought I saw
gnawing on a glove that had a tail,
nor the coyote loping past, trying
to look dog-harmless.

Nor the geese that used to squawk,
circle the lake, and crap on everyone
and everything under their flight path.
They were culled, their meat given
to soup kitchens, victims of climate change
when winters became too mild
for them to migrate back north.

No crocodile that turned out
to be an urban legend, nor the bear
that rode a Ferris wheel
on the northwest edge of the city:

Nothing that made us gasp and point,
just a pleasant park morning,
a soothing breeze, cottony clouds-wisps,
acquaintances waving hello,
all of us wishing each other
a good, uneventful day.

Robert Cooperman
Denver, Colorado

Just a Bite

1) Eve

    A second wife, a second chance. You were never given any such reprieve. You did not know of the lies of the snake and the uncaring nature of the maker. You did not realize it cruel to be tested of such a dichotomy when you knew not of good or evil—until you tasted the flesh and your eyes opened. In that moment, what did pure and unfiltered knowledge taste like?

    (All she wanted was a fig)

2) Persephone

    Homer described you as formidable. True, your teeth were like knives as you took your bite, ruby seeds tumbling from your lips—Hades thought the juice was blood on your chin. He kissed you and all he could taste was sweetness. How did you hide the sharpness of your being so well?

    (All she wanted was a pomegranate)

3) Izanami

    You had circled the pillar of heaven with your love. You were supposed to live eternally in the sunrisen lands. And so, wrapped in death with no hope of rescue, all you wanted was brightness for your eyes and sweetness for the tip of your tongue. You ate, teeth sinking deep regardless of what it meant. Was it the juice staining your kimono, or your newly rotting flesh?

    (All she wanted was a persimmon)

4) Xochiquetzal

    You were not even able to taste it, before the tree split in two and suddenly you were alone. Juice still stained your fingertips, the fragrance the last remembrance of paradise. The sun had never been so bright, though the world was now so dark. It reminded you of that ill fated fruit, of the sweetness of paradise. Would it all have been worth it if you had only been able to take a bite?

    (All she wanted was a passionfruit)

5) Idunn

    Golden and bright, youth eternal in your arms as you harvested the forest's bounty. You were lured from home with a promise of your interests, by tricksters and ice covered

giants. But without you, youth will not last for those left across the rainbow bridge. When you were captured, did you weep for yourself or for the aging?
(All she wanted was an apple)

Lilian Bodley
Moscow, Idaho

Our City

Back in the city with the all-night subways
and all that
I'm sure your young city is just as energetic
I was so relaxed
finally having solved every question
except love and self-love of course

Now daily it's lights-out again so quickly
with not a single check having been marked
in the list I created way way way back
It was the only thing I arrived carrying
to the great city
She left a space for it in our super-stuffed
suitcase when we left

You'll leave yours too
when you finally realize you'll never
be smart enough for it
I thank her still for coming with me
and asking me no questions

Steven Ray Smith
Austin, Texas

Northern Ringneck

Crucified between plastic garbage bins in the garage,
it died young—four inches—
wearing a necklace the color of beach sand
lit against night-black of its back.

A spider—uncertain type—rested on its skull,
one head feasting on the other.

What else might I define as terror
than the small devoured by the smaller?

All in nature plays a form of predator.
I've witnessed this on wildlife shows
in which a cheetah stalks the youngest stray gazelle,
something has gored a lion with its tusks,
cobra spits venom at the camera's lens,

yet didn't anticipate the wilderness in a void
between receptacles. Walls & doors
won't keep the cult of death at prayer for long.

Ace Boggess
Charleston, West Virginia

Childhood Enrichment

This was back in the seventies when you could do this
and not be charged with childhood endangerment,

I'd throw both kids in the back seat,
a couple of old blankets, and drive.

Down the darkest, longest country road, not stopping
until we couldn't see a single light in any direction.

We'd spread one blanket on the warm hood of the car,
climb up, snuggle together, and pull the other atop us.

Watching for meteors—shooting stars—
too many and too fast to even wish on one!

And even though it was a school night, all thoughts
of homework and bedtimes were left far behind.

Sometimes we would wake up with the sun on our faces,
having fallen asleep counting the stars as they whizzed by,

only the three of us in the whole universe, and the stars
whispering their lullabies throughout the night.

Charlene Neely
Lincoln, Nebraska

Holly, Who Works Overnights at the Kwik Shop

she's robbed—twice—between midnight and 5am
42 dollars and some change
thought she'd never see her son again
or her disabled mom
the cops keep her for hours
same questions over and over
she just wants to get home
see her son before school
they finally let her go
Rhonda is her shift relief—
gives her the report, tells her to be careful
be back at 11pm for her shift
hope it's just the usual crowd
for beer and smokes
or that one guy who hangs outside
smokes weed by the air pumps
keeps an eye on the place
gives her the good stuff
to get her through the night

Cathy Porter
Omaha, Nebraska

The Attic

Tapestries of gossamer
festoon rough-hewn rafters.
Knotty old floorboards
groan under a century's burden of
memories, dust-coated secrets,
buried shadows in decaying chests,
hearts stilled and gone frigid.

A shaft of skittish sunbeams
pierces a grimy window,
spotlighting crazed sepias
of austere gentlemen
in over-starched high collars
and ladies bedecked
in lacy décolletage
and frilly hats, looking
quite prim and proper.

In a dank, dusty corner
where the sun never visits
a doll lies long-abandoned,
naked, crumpled, eyes
rolled back in a face
of fractured china.

Krikor N. Der Hohannesian
Medford, Massachusetts

Beginning

The nurse appeared to bathe him during the hour
my mother was gone for groceries. Like a child,
he hid behind me, curled as a cocktail shrimp.

No other woman had ever seen him naked,
but the nurse, kind as she was, wouldn't wait.
He placed himself in her hands, allowed her

to prop him mannequin-like against Travertine,
wipe clean his retired sex, the thinning white pelt
of his chest. Soon after, Mother returned,

with milk, to find him scrubbed, and dazed
from missing her. He hadn't missed her in ages.

Katherine Fallon
Statesboro, Georgia

Blue Dress Wearing a Small Girl

Between the singled socks,
lost slippers, snuck-candy wrappers,
dust warrens
under the bed,

the blue dress smooths its white apron,
wonders why we don't drink tea anymore—

pinkies out,
paper party hat unicorning great-grandfather.
Curating piquant notes:
    freon in the pink pot (ventside)
    magnolia, from the open window, in the green

The blue dress wore the small girl first,
then it wore a stuffed hippo-bear.

The blue dress liked the hippo-bear,
even when its fur rubbed off,
but the hippo-bear went on a diet—
raisined up and spewed fluffy brains
until the blue dress couldn't wear it anymore, either.

Karisma J. Tobin
Houston, Texas

No True Dark

At any hour of the night in the apartments
that surround ours, there is a light on.
Strangers are up and about, digging
through refrigerators and reading books.

I feel kinship with these people, largely unseen
except for their light, their movement.

I am up with my child tonight, but I have been
up with my body lately, that un-named knife
in my gut causing problems.

When I lived in a house, I would go out on the
porch swing with my sleeplessness and envy the
street full of dark windows.

Caitlin Thomson
Toronto, Ontario, Canada

Summer Haibun

(at Crown Cove Beach)

This summer's long light fills with bright lemons, melons, corn, all the silken thoughts. It languishes under a splashy beach umbrella with dominoes and Scrabble, with children digging fingers and toes into sand where facets of sunlight bead cascades along windy waves, run of shorebirds sweeping the horizon before the gray cityscape.

This summer is for a young mother jostling her baby in low tide
as we doze off on the soft lull of water lapping the shore, under the
    cirrus
feathered sky in oncoming sunset. This is the time of day when
    curtains billow
at windows in soft light, when sun squints through above a rippling
    bay,
when summer knocks at the door and we answer,

                              the wail of seagulls
                              winging wild above a catch
                              eyes fixed past us

Andrena Zawinski
Alameda, California

Early Friday I Wondered, Suddenly, Was Cab Calloway Living, Was He Dead

leaped to the Boardwalk where my mother had us
waiting in line for a chance to see his
crinkly *Hi De Ho* laugh tho my sister and I
wanted to feel the salt wind lick us like
sailors' eyes, safe in the leash of our
mother's sighs no matter how tight my sarong

dress of aqua and jade leaves like one my
mother would pick out when she couldn't
still walk, let alone think of shimmying to
Minnie the Moocher, only got it after making
me try it on saying she couldn't even be buried
in it. Salt wind and lights like rhinestones

and diamond as unlike the room she left when
she was hostage to my sister's bossiness, *her*
perfect body, tiny and blonde as we grew like
flowers my mother over-watered, wild to make
sure nothing died, now spreading beyond even her
biggest clothes as she plotted to keep the sun

dress she could never wear that July when she
helped my mother out on an ambulance ride south.
But that June we were teens, my sister wrapped
in dreams of races and jockeys like Willie Shoe
maker and I in my even smaller sleek clothes
were herded in to hear this man who wiggled as much
as Elvis. Our mother's hair, black fire shaking, maybe
46 or 47—too old we figured then to be so taken by Cab's
flirty eyes, his scat hinting at what *our* mother couldn't
imagine we were sure, let alone want

Lyn Lifshin
Vienna, Virginia

Who's Who

In a New York restaurant
I'm waited on
by an out-of-work actor
while the cook
is a wannabe playwright
and the busboy directs plays
in his dreams.

The guy that cuts my hair
is a poet.
The New Yorker can't recognize
genius when they see it.
And the Uber driver's writing
the great American novel.
At least, he would be
if his work hours weren't so long.
As for this woman I'm dating…
she's strictly renaissance.
An actor, director, playwright,
poet, playwright, novelist,
that I met at a Duane Reade register.
She was the one
with the warm, engaging smile
who scanned my bar codes.

In the city,
I run into so many people
who are something other
than what they seem to be.
I buy coffee
from the next great rap star.
The most amazing of all undiscovered voices
belongs to the kebob guy
who parks on my block.

But then there's a cop
who's happy enough
just walking his beat.

He's lucky he's a cop.
Around here,
living out your dreams
could get a guy arrested.

John Grey
Johnston, Rhode Island

Even Out Back, I'd Travel with a Trowel

Mambas move, bejeweled bangles in tall grass.
    Though I've never been to Sub-Saharan Africa,

I know they're there. I've heard they drop
    from the trees like unfurled tires.

You make me think of them when I look you
    in the eyes and you smile poison-bright.

Mamba, rat snake, it's all the same: what's prey,
    how you circle dreys and other safe spaces.

I can pinpoint your slither into sacred temples,
    your passage over cool stone and while you

might be blessed there alone, these are not
    the gods I worship.

My mind keeps going back to the nest
    I found this cold January:

three small squirrels spooning, deep sleep, dreaming,
    which makes me realize I never write

about squirrels because "squirrels" is a word
    that demands humor and this is deadly serious

as defined by your lidless eyes and sinuous disaster.
    You've got no scruples, you'll engorge yourself,

disregarding the soft fur and the quiet wonder
    of breath taken.

See, you squirm closer. See, you open your jaw—
    imagine the needle bright bite.

And imagine I strike, slit you down the middle, let you
    flip headless in the death throes of your greed.

Christine Butterworth-McDermott
Nacogdoches, Texas

For Mary Oliver

Glancing down there are succulents by my feet
Curling with mathematical precision
Something so small, is this
What Fibonacci saw?
The universe spiralling infinite inward

You died two days ago
And everyone, everywhere, is struck by you
The woods filled with poets as the winter sun dips
My wild and precious life simmering sparking
Ever more vibrant under my skin

Walking I have to stop because
Behind the blue is the endless dark and
I can feel myself spinning through emptiness
Can Ann still feel her fireworks heart sounding out from Voyager, now?
Every moment of beauty arcing away and back through years and light

If I die today, here, now
If the last thing I see is the whirling sky and
The air is never sweet in my lungs again and
I never kiss her again
It would still be an egregious sin to feel anything but gratitude for having been here at all

But I will sin anyway
Every time the forest floor numbs my curled toes
Every bloodied moon and every ache
Even heartsick, sleepless, lonely
I will ask, I will demand it, as the prophets say:
More Life

Sasha Blakeley
North Vancouver, British Columbia, Canada

New Roots

Soft leaves, so small,
Cluster on newly naked
Stems. Let water bathe and
Caress each vulnerability.
Let sun breathe on them.

Growth will come. Don't let
This slowness burden you.
You've decided it's time.
That is enough for now.
Don't watch for every sign.

We draw our own connections.
A bounty of light rushes in,
Darkness too. Allows it to happen.
No visible tap root, revelations
Come where we're most open.

Roots will form again
When it's time. Trust
Nature's agenda, now that
You've helped it surely along—
You can only force so much.

Karen Poppy
San Anselmo, California

What She Knows

She thinks about the two-piece
she wants to wear during summer.
She'll be told to put on clothes
before she leaves the pool, while the boys
still drip onto the hot pavement.

She learns that as a black girl, the only thing
more dangerous than wearing a two-piece
bathing suit down the street is asking
to wear one down the street because
black parents think that when a black girl
is asking, it's because she wants to be seen.
They never see it as an innocent question
by a girl that just wants to wear a two-piece.

Because to ask is to acknowledge that there
Is a swelling of want for her to explore.
To be the girl they knew she would become.
The one who would embrace the same
sins as the black girls before her.
It's her job to be a judge.
She's supposed to know when shorts are too short,
bra straps too visible, when girls her own age
are too promiscuous.

What a dangerous line she treads in those
summer days when the only thing stopping
her from being a sinful black girl,
is learning how to recognize that behavior
in other black girls.

Princess Zuri' McCann
Hamden, Connecticut

Lingering

For that which has died
and been laid to rest
deep in my chest
in the cavern of a fist
and the pit of my stomach
never to flow in or out
or to be digested
as it digests
me from the inside
and remains there.

The thing about mortality
Is that we are susceptible
To the vacuum around us
That leaves but an empty husk
Of memories that we come to dissect
The only part of us that breathes
Through our lying teeth
Through our paper lungs
That clings like a second skin.

Julia Horensten
Orlando, Florida

Unwritten

I'll start with unlicking the envelope seal,
to take back secrets the letter conceals

in straightening quarter folds into
three pages. I'll pry out the corner staple,
the paper molded around punctures
I iron out with the flat of my nail,
and pull apart each page, each blue and red,
college ruled line. I'll tape serrated edges

back into the notebook and push the ball
in the socket of my pen to roll
back the ink I placed on this page, the heart words
I'll take back for a stubbed toe and wrong directions,
so you could never hear my harsh words
and undo our friendship in rejection.

Danielle Valverde
Lincoln, Nebraska

A Monologue of a Theater Teacher

I go and break the Proscenium fourth wall
almost every day after I have my 3 o'clock
Starbucks blonde roast, no sugar, no creamer.
Students know me as I know them
But only if they could realize the horror,
Of knowing everyone by their first and last
name. I wouldn't be teaching this class
I would be in every movie and TV show
reciting the names on the credits, but
then I would not sleep at night.
In a fighting scene there should be
only two people, give and take, act and response,
but three people bring in all the confusion.

Sujash Purna
Springfield, Missouri

The Problem with Water

                I saw myself off into color,
                warm peach-flesh leaves
And raw bulls-blood red amid the drought-hit greens.
Whole fields of yellow mustard, knee-high, lit the ground
Too dry for harvest.
           And the corn fields too,
this year, have been too whiskery for running,
Brown surrounding blades slapping hard, breaking
Far too easy.
        I try not to worry that the apples
Don't taste sweet this year, even the honeycrisp,
The fuji, the goldenacre.
                It does not work to try.
In the steel mesh bowl sit apples we gathered, together
Before driving home across dry plains—a place
That saw a flood not long ago.

B. Neal Kirchner
Palmyra, Nebraska

Some Things I've Not Done

I've not killed the perpetrator
I've not stood outside his house
    brick wrapped in parchment
I've not sent cash to the outposts
I've not told my daughters
I've not sold everything
I've not knelt
I've not risen above it
I've not planted
    or flaunted
I've not engaged my neighbor
I've not said here, you can sleep in my bed
I've not traced the names on the wall
I've not brought matches

What I have done

I have made more lists
I have begun to weep

                              Florence Weinberger
                              Malibu, California

Almost August

On the patio
in a folding chair

with sweat bees
cicadas
and the panting dog

sixty-seven summers
swamp my mind

with mummified months
in the old back yard

the sticky darkness
of matinees

campfire, bug bite
chlorine, lotion
and smooth hot skin,

my young legs stretched
from a bathing suit
without an end
in sight.

Michael Lyle
Purcellville, Virginia

Comfort at the Muzzleloader Café, Billings, Montana

On battered blackboards, all day breakfast,
Polish sausages and kraut, $7.99.

A flat lock muzzleloader, harnesses and tack
displayed on walls, with fifty-year-old pictures
of the rodeo in town.

Marty tucks up to the table, scans the menu
for his favorite steak. *Remember when—*

*—you know the one who died on Grandma's birthday,
so cold, was only 10 degrees—we had to shovel snow.*

Photos of cowboys, cattle drives, the wagon train,
pails and coal hobs, and a clean two-ended full buck saw.

*When was that year?—before the oil, before
they found the Indian caves.*

We eat chicken fried steak, iceberg lettuce
decked with olives, grated cheese and whole wheat rolls.

Marty gazes, fills himself with bread.

Linda Conroy
Bellingham, Washington

I Ask My Realtor How to Keep the Ghosts the Same

I live in houses and meet ghosts who learn to live with me.
They don't ask why I'm here. I don't ask how they died.
We sit together the first week, watch Dateline. Each night
they count the breaths I take between sleep and wake

In the morning I count the breaths beneath their sheet.
We lie, say the number is the same.
When I turn the key, when I leave
they stay. I move houses, the ghosts change.

Megan Mary Moore
Cincinnati, Ohio

Cradle of Moss

Summer heat pushed
thin mirror-waves
above asphalt
that ended
at the leaf-mat path.
It spread and curved
under the shadow
of sentinel trees.
The green side of them
needled north,
they were an escort beyond
walls, and cars, and dogs.

This morning
the songbirds call—
then it is calm,
then nothing at all.
Afternoon there is only
the dove's coo,
and stream-waters
licking rocks.
They flow around
the pronged bend
with its perfect cradle
of moss; this place
of leaving off.

Kathrine M. Cays
New Hill, North Carolina

My Foolish Heart

Bill Evans and Oscar Peterson
are in my kitchen
sound waves travel through my astral body
telling me,
 I Got it Bad—Ain't That Good.
It's as close to God as I can get,
imagining at St. Peter's gates
 OP is playing *Night & Day.*

 For Heaven's Sake, I
can feel it in my bones
 sidereal time in these deep-skied stars
I am holy now *'Cause*
 Spring is Here
Oh, How My Heart Sings, Bill.

And if the seven horns of heaven
are sounding, let it be
Satchmo, Buddy, Cannonball & Nat
 I Loves You, Miles
  I Loves You, Blackbird.

The holiest people ever die from drugs
and I hear his fingers move
 across the keys
The pipes, the pipes are calling.
Death can take so much but
 here I am
And Bill tells me,
  It's Time For Love,
  If You Could Only See Me Now.

       Abigail Warren
     Northampton, Massachusetts

Survey

I shine a light against
the leaves.   no good.
behind the darkness I hear
the grinding of a wooden
frog   like you'd buy
at a music festival.
ridges along the spine
& mallet in its mouth.
make make make
sound I'm hearing:
raccoon fighting
some poor domestic
    whining thing
        passing

of windshield wipers
& the dust in the hinges.
a branch drips down
from the leaves spilling
over the power line
    woman inside
        & her blow dryer.
    honestly,
tell me how come

you've never thought
of leaf hair? I can't be
the first to have seen
someone holding it up:
big green elephant ear
still wet with it
    self, crunching
only under pressure,
I saw water reflecting
chlorophyll colors,
water that I had breathed.

                                Jonce Marshall Palmer
                                Tallahassee, Florida

Pink Wheat

Even as pressure is lifted
from middle C, the note will still linger
out here, blasting from the steering
wheel and deep into the bones,
the toes. Scarecrows
are rising once again, striking
at the feathered sky and soiling
the sun with their stitchling
smiles. Legend has it that they will evolve
from gingham to silk in a matter
of hours. Their button-eyes ask,
is this really running away?
Ahead, a man has pulled over to photograph
the halted locomotive. He clutches
the camera and a heathered sweater ever
closer. The vulture tornado twists
above you, and you're nestled
within this grainy horizon.
You are running away,
ground bowing as you take each step,
pressure coming again,
stifled blasts. Look up: the clouds have veins
and all is stalled,
like this.

Anna Ciummo
Seattle, Washington

I Wish I Had Batman's Origin Story

I'm from blossom blizzards in a peach orchard fairyland,
Ditches that swallow up my hot pink Barbie Jeep,
Visits to the principal's office after flashing Jack my chi-chis,
Blue-tweed couch cushion trampolines, and private
Powerline concerts at the end of an old VCR tape.

I'm from two months in Texas to get away from
a loaded magnum patriarch, only to return by the whim of
a sell out with a wine glass glued to her hand,
Nothing but a blank sheet of paper to turn in for Father's Day.

I'm from an empty stomach for three days because
"You'd look so pretty if you lost some weight,"
Thanking my grandmother for her concern, while
she orders us Mountain Mikes with extra cheese.

I'm from my mom's .38 special in my hands while she's at work,
The kids at school all hate me because I'm a curve-breaker,
packed-down ceiling texture friends behind a locked bedroom door,
tinnitus from Blink-182 blaring in my over-ears because
Mark Hoppus is the only one that understood.

Keli Lindsey
Riverbank, California

Richard's Story

Richard was telling us how he came to live
in High Falls, and it all seemed to have
something to do with stepping on a dog
and killing it, a black poodle on a black floor

that he didn't see, though I missed something
of the story, because I don't know where
it happened or what he was doing there, just
that it left the woman owner hysterical, and

somehow caused Richard to move to High Falls,
46 years ago now, and Richard was laughing
as he told the story and we were laughing, though
the dog had died and its owner was distraught,

all of that decades ago, and, really, I missed something
of the story, so now, even though I was laughing,
and someone suggested Richard's story was worthy
of a poem, I don't know if it should be happy or sad.

Matthew J. Spireng
Kingston, New York

Buzz

Now post war, there is concern about the bees,
or even if a swarm is still in the hedgerow.

Shyly, I rub bee balm on my wrist, shout
zee-ee through the house. Some say I am not

well. Who knows if I fade in and out
of a hive. Best sit, weep my way to spring.

For the queen gone, a tank cutting too close
to the hedgerow. O *zee-ee*, what buzz

will keep me alive. For am I not
the keeper to lead the wounded of wing

back to the hive. Am I not the mourner,
there at the hedgerow. O *zee-ee,*

I need the fat bee with pollen on its belly
I need the jar of honey on the window

sill. Else I stay and stay in the burnt-out
hive. I need the buzz to stay alive.

Mary Ann Meade
Lansdowne, Pennsylvania

www.ingramcontent.com/pod-product-compliance
Lightning Source LLC
Chambersburg PA
CBHW030155100526
44592CB00009B/294